Tuning In

Also by Robert Maidment

Straight Talk: A Guide to Saying More With Less (1983)
Robert's Rules of Disorder: A Guide to Mismanagement (1976)
Simulation Games: Design and Implementation (1973)
Criticism, Conflict, and Change (1970)

Tuning In
A Guide To Effective Listening

ROBERT MAIDMENT

PELICAN PUBLISHING COMPANY
GRETNA 1984

Copyright © 1984
By Robert Maidment
All rights reserved

*To those who listen well now
and to others who will listen better later*

Library of Congress Cataloging in Publication Data

Maidment, Robert.
　Tuning in.

　　1. Listening.　I. Title.
BF323.L5M35　1984　　　153.6　　　84-5259
ISBN 0-88289-439-0

Manufactured in the United States of America

Published by Pelican Publishing Company, Inc.
1101 Monroe Street, Gretna, Louisiana 70053

Contents

Preface, 9

Listening
 Skill
 No.

1	Acknowledge the Miracle, 15
2	First, Find a Listener, 16
3	Listen—Really Listen, 17
4	Learn to Listen Better, 19
5	Engage the Brain, 20
6	Show Regard for Your Listener, 21
7	Take Time to Listen, 22
8	"Listen to Me!"—a Primitive View, 23
9	"Listen to Me!"—a Less Primitive View, 25
10	"Listen to Me!"—a Still Less Primitive View, 27
11	Discriminate Among Sounds, 28
12	Adjust Attitudes Before Applying Skills, 29
13	Check Emotional Levels, 30
14	Rate Your Own Listening Skill, 31
15	Note Your Listening Traits, 33
16	Check Your Patterns, 35
17	Respect Your Audience, 36
18	Know What You Want, 37
19	Count Numbers Because Numbers Count, 39
20	Regard Old Messages as New Ones, 40
21	Listen First, Then Answer, 41
22	Don't Blame Your Listener, 42
23	Respect Listener Differences, 43
24	Listen Carefully, 44
25	Listen for Ideas, 45
26	Acknowledge the Consequences of Not Listening, 47
27	Listen Smarter, 48
28	Listen Silently, 49

Listening
Skill
No.

29	Interpret Paralanguage,	50
30	Respect Attention Spans,	51
31	Include Us All in Conversation,	52
32	Repeat What You Hear,	53
33	Guard Against Drifting,	54
34	Mind Your Manner,	55
35	Select Your Listening Space,	57
36	Listen for Feelings and Reduce Costs,	59
37	Unclutter Your Speech,	60
38	See More, Hear More,	61
39	Say More, Hear More,	62
40	Consider the Arena,	63
41	Engage Your Listener Gently,	64
42	Avoid Compulsive Talkers,	65
43	Question Unclear Signals,	66
44	Listen for Meaning,	67
45	Listen to Know,	69
46	Listen Carefully to Your Tapes,	70
47	Reduce the Signals,	71
48	Avoid Noise Pollution When You Can,	72
49	Reduce Noise Pollution When You Can't Avoid It,	73
50	When You Can't Hear, Say So,	74
51	Case the Space,	75
52	Match the Message with the Medium,	77
53	Know When to Talk,	78
54	Provide Specific Information,	79
55	Indulge the Diverters,	80
56	Hear Ye! The Eyes Have It,	81
57	Be at Ease with Those Wearing Bright Feathers,	82
58	Insist Upon Two-Way Exchanges,	83
59	Beware of Distortions,	84
60	Muzzle Those Who Roar,	85
61	Listen—If at First You Don't Heed, Hear Again,	86
62	Interrupt Whenever Necessary,	87
63	Remember the Pain,	88
64	Deflate the Flatulent,	89
65	Try Mnemonics,	90
66	Listen to Those Who Know,	91

Listening
Skill
No.

67	Hear Not, Heed Not, 92
68	Be Wary of Extended Silences, 93
69	Digest the Dry and the Difficult, 94
70	Beware of Lionizing Body Language, 95
71	Acknowledge the Distinction Between the Medium and the Message, 96
72	Reduce the Effort, Increase the Reward, 97
73	Avoid Heavy Winds and Dense Fog, 98
74	Laugh and Listen, 99
75	Exercise Care with Arousal Words, 100
76	Be There to Hear, 101
77	Listen—and Live, 102
78	Assess the Odds, 103
79	Help Yourself, 105
80	Help the Speaker, 107
81	Adopt Listening Skills for Lifetime Use, 109
82	Market Listening—It Pays!, 110
83	Practice Today for Proficiency Tomorrow, 111
84	Probe Periodically, 112

Preface

*From listening comes wisdom—
From talking, repentance.*

Italian proverb

Most of us listen inefficiently. We are willing victims of the Listening Law of Three-Fourths:

> Three-fourths of the time we spend awake each workday is consumed by talking and listening activity;
> Three-fourths of what we do hear, we hear imprecisely; and
> Three-fourths of what we hear accurately, we forget within three weeks.

Although listening is the most often used communicative skill, we've been given the least training in it.

This volume is a repentant confession that I've not always been a good listener. These concepts, divergencies, musings, speculations, and ramblings are notes on the nature of listening extracted from what we "hear" happening when people converse. On each page a specific listening skill is described. Readers are invited to apply personal meaning to those items which, if practiced, could either enhance their listening ability or enable someone else to listen more effectively.

If, as author John D. MacDonald suggests, "a good listener is more rare than an adequate lover," perhaps our pursuit of preciseness in listening is futile. However, with a heightened awareness of faulty listening habits, our appreciation for good listening increases as well. As we strive to improve both our receptive and our expressive skills, opportunities for minimizing misunderstandings increase.

PREFACE

The end product of listening is knowing. Here is what I now "know" about listening—or, recasting another Italian phrase, I came, I heard, I concurred. Perhaps you will also.

Acknowledgments

For permission to quote from *The Medusa and the Snail: More Notes of A Biology Watcher* by Lewis Thomas. Copyright © 1979 by Lewis Thomas. Reprinted by permission of Viking Penguin Inc. For permission to reprint the communication chart, page 18, The Sperry Corporation, © 1983. And an appreciation for the words of Richard Bandler, Alexander Graham Bell, Joy Blake, Madelyn Burley-Allen, Victor Borge, Philip Bruschi, Julius Caesar, Johnny Carson, Calvin Coolidge, Peter Drucker, Thomas A. Edison, Albert Ellis, Ralph Waldo Emerson, W. C. Fields, Carlos Fuentes, Samuel Goldwyn, John Grinder, Edward T. Hall, E. F. Hutton, Jack Kerouac, R. D. Laing, John Lavach, Walter Lord, Merrill Lynch, John D. MacDonald, Steve Martin, Marshall McLuhan, Samuel F. B. Morse, Edward R. Murrow, Clark E. Moustakas, Billy Packer, Rosemary Potter, Theodore Reik, Wilbur Schramm, Al Smith, Jonathan Swift, Mark Twain, Arnold Toynbee, Kurt Vonnegut, Jr., John Wayne, Norbert Weiner, and Ron Wheeler.

Tuning In

LISTENING SKILL NO. 1
Acknowledge the Miracle

The Action

This is a small book about how we listen. It is not a book about how we hear. The detecting of vibratory signals, tones, pitches, rhythms, and motions remains for me a truly spellbinding process. We won't, therefore, be discussing tympanic membranes or eustachian tubes. Instead, we will be exploring a myriad of situational variables that affect listening. Hearing is one miracle; really listening to what we say to each other is another.

The Replay

On the development of the human brain:

> One cell is switched on to become the whole trillioncell massive apparatus for thinking and imagining and, for that matter, being surprised. No one has a ghost of an idea how this works. If anyone ever does succeed in explaining it.... I will charter a skywriting airplane, maybe a whole fleet of them, and send them aloft to write one great exclamation point after another around the whole sky until my money runs out.
>
> —Lewis Thomas
> *The Medusa and the Snail*

LISTENING SKILL NO. 2
First, Find a Listener

The Action

To be heard I need a listener. Your presence suggests only a physical state. Perhaps you don't want to listen to me now—or later, either. You want to be doing something else. Ignoring your need, I persist in talking, and you in turn continue ignoring me and listening to nothing. Similarly, a man winks at a woman in a dark room. He knows what he's doing but she doesn't. A message sent is not always a message received. Having something to say to someone having no inclination to listen is worse than having nothing to say and saying it.

The Replay

If a person isn't communicating, the least he can do is remain silent.

LISTENING SKILL NO. 3
Listen—Really Listen

The Action

Listening is sensing. It goes beyond hearing or assessing only the spoken words. Listening is committing. It goes beyond recalling previous conversations or continuing a dialogue simply because it's convenient to do so. Listening is caring. It goes beyond impersonal verbal exchanges or faking attention when we'd prefer to do something else. Listening requires that a virtual transfusion take place: for given moments two become one and neither can be quite the same again. Listening—focused, sensitive, interactive, and responsive—is a most remarkable but severely underutilized creative force.

The Replay

... a transfusion takes place; he is you and you are he—and by no unfriendly chance or bad company can he ever quite lose the benefit.

—Ralph Waldo Emerson

COMMUNICATION SKILL	WHEN LEARNED	EXTENT USED	EXTENT TAUGHT
Listening	1st	45%	4th
Speaking	2nd	30%	3rd
Reading	3rd	16%	2nd
Writing	4th	9%	1st

LISTENING SKILL NO. 4
Learn to Listen Better

The Action

Executives of the Sperry Corporation, the company that "understands how important it is to listen," claim that while listening is the most often used basic communication skill, it is the one least often taught (see table at left).

We're aware that we spend much of our time processing sounds—invited and uninvited, rhapsodic and raucous, clear and cloudy, inspirational and insipid. Not so apparent, however, is the fact that we invest precious little time learning how to tune in, sort out, attend to, extract from, talk about, and recall what we do hear.

The Replay

Listening: "the neglected communication skill"—Philip Bruschi

Listening: "the forgotten skill"—Madelyn Burley-Allen

Listening: "the least understood of the communications arts"—Robert L. Montgomery

Listening: "the overlooked and underdeveloped other half of talking"—Ron Wheeler

Listening: apparently the skill people haven't heard enough about.

LISTENING SKILL NO. 5
Engage the Brain

The Action

Although words reach us at 1100 feet per second, we process them at 186,000 miles per second. Slow talking speed impedes our fast thinking capability. My mental computer "downtime" between your words, sentences, and ideas permits various patterns of inattention. Obviously, the disparity between talk speed and think speed cannot be bridged by faster speaking or slower listening. As listeners, we can use our mental downtime to replay, review, and refine all incoming messages. While hearing may be fast and physical, listening is methodical and mental.

The Replay

Communication is the act of the recipient—the sender utters

—PETER DRUCKER

LISTENING SKILL NO. 6
Show Regard for Your Listener

The Action

In any conversation, I convey my actual degree of liking for you, my perceived degree of control over you, and my current receptivity to what you say. The fondness and forcefulness factors are heavily determined by my values and our prior exchanges. The receptivity factor is less restrictive. During short exchanges I can learn to receive, regard, and respond to what anyone thinks or feels. Now I'm helping others help me understand them.

The Replay

I just tell myself to listen with affection to anyone who talks to me, to be in their shoes when they talk; to try to know them without my mind pressing against theirs, or arguing, or changing the subject.

—Clark E. Moustakas

LISTENING SKILL NO. 7
Take Time to Listen

The Action

If we're only sharing information, the exchange can be quick and brief. A Merrill Lynch commodity maxim appropriately concurs: "It's not just how much you know. It's how soon." If, however, we want to explore friendships, check out hunches, tune in to feelings, or develop better working relationships, then we must invest sufficient time in the exchange. Good listening doesn't just happen. It takes time. And patience. And sensitivity. And skill. And ... say, how much more time do we have anyway?

The Replay

The obscure we see eventually, the completely apparent takes longer.

—EDWARD R. MURROW

LISTENING SKILL NO. 8
"Listen to Me!"—a Primitive View

The Action

We frequently encounter others who retain naive notions regarding communication. This lingering, primitive view suggests that once I've spoken, it's up to you to get the message.

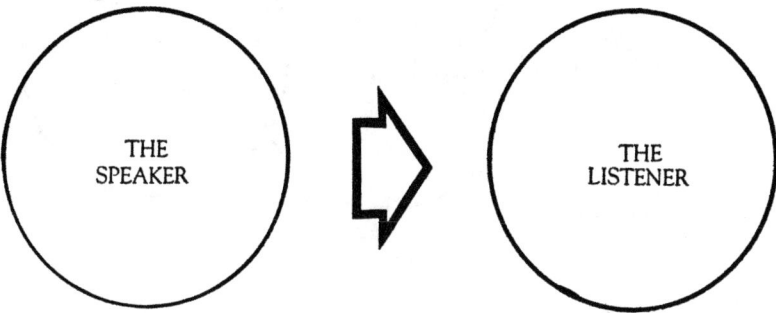

The naive model rests upon several assumptions often made by speakers about listeners:

1. The listener can hear.
2. The listener is listening.
3. The listener wants to hear what you say.
4. The listener understands what you say.
5. The listener will act as you wish in response to the information received.
6. The listener remains passive while the speaker with a message to deliver takes an active or dominant role.

When one or more of these assumptions is inoperative, faulty communication is guaranteed.

The Replay

I've told you what I want you to know. Since you heard what I said, you now know what I know and how I feel.

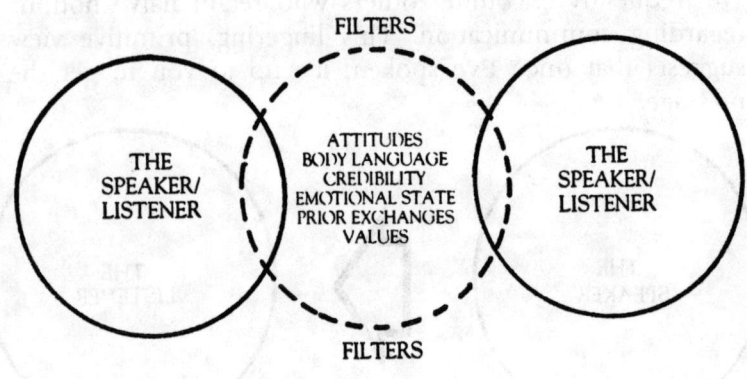

LISTENING SKILL NO. 9
"Listen to Me!"—a Less Primitive View

The Action

Those who study the interaction between speaker and listener usually acknowledge a filtering phenomenon. Our attitudes, emotions, and values pass through and are distorted by others' perceptual screens or filters when messages are exchanged (see illustration at left).

This communications model rests upon certain supportable assumptions:

1. Communication is a two-way process requiring a "partnership" between speaker and listener.
2. Because of ever-present distortion, messages need to be checked and confirmed.
3. Since messages convey both thoughts and feelings, effective communication involves both.

When these assumptions become operational, the quality of an interaction is enhanced.

The Replay

While we've been talking and listening, we've reviewed and clarified each other's words and feelings. Although I still don't know precisely what your real message is, nor you mine, we're continuing to explore—and enjoying our differences whenever possible.

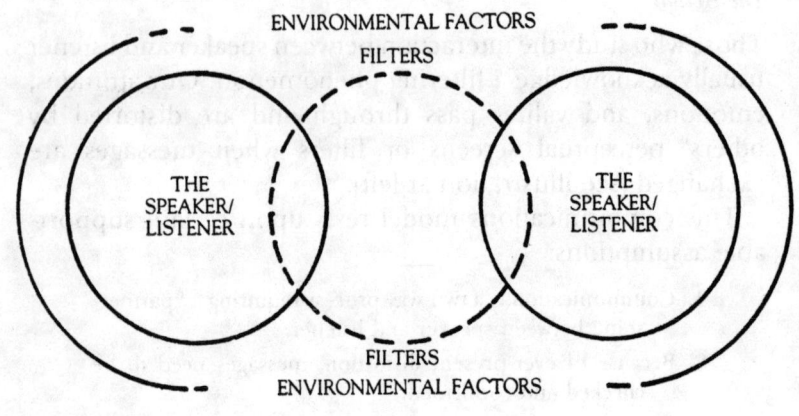

LISTENING SKILL NO. 10
"Listen to Me!"—a Still Less Primitive View

The Action

Yet another view of the speaker-listener relationship includes such environmental factors as acoustics, distractions, proximity, a real or perceived audience, and the amount of time available for a given interaction as well as its location (see illustration at left).

The word "primitive" has been used to describe these models because the art of communication is ever-changing. Current studies of certain psychic phenomena, body chemistry processes, circadian rhythms, right/left brain relationships, and personal wellness patterns will yield additional data, providing an expanded stage and setting for our communications.

The Replay

   I wanted to give my language a body.

>   —CARLOS FUENTES,
>   Novelist Turned Playwright

LISTENING SKILL NO. 11
Discriminate Among Sounds

The Action

Close your eyes for one minute. Sixty seconds. Now.

What did you hear? Your own breathing? Ventilation equipment? Traffic? Crickets? Nothing? Do it again, but this time *listen*. Count the number of identifiable sounds. Do it now.

Was there a difference? We can monitor sounds more effectively. We can select certain stimulating, alerting, or enchanting noises while ignoring others. Muffle the mundane and savor the significant. The choice is ours.

The Replay

Rural visitor to city friend at busy intersection: Listen—a cricket!
City friend: Nonsense, there are no crickets around here.
Visitor (dropping a quarter): Listen.
Several heads turn at the sound.
Visitor: See, you hear a quarter. I hear a cricket. We listen differently.

LISTENING SKILL NO. 12
Adjust Attitudes Before Applying Skills

The Action

A venerable truism suggests that it's not what you say, it's *how* you say it. And while our phone company implores us to "reach out and touch someone," the attitudes of both speaker and listener can profoundly distort messages. Even if we refine our listening skills, ultimate mastery is undermined when our attitude toward someone, the topic under discussion, or memories of another situation color (and thereby distort) what we hear. Only when we acknowledge our attitudes can we apply our technical listening skills systematically and successfully, so that phone visit can truly be "the next best thing to being there."

The Replay

The dumb things you do speak so loudly that I can't hear what you say!

LISTENING SKILL NO. 13
Check Emotional Levels

The Action

Among the different factors that influence and thereby distort messages between a speaker and a listener is the emotional state of either. Our moods affect word choice, voice tone, and body language. While the official agenda—the actual topic of conversation—appears to be totally rational, the unofficial agenda—the internal body chemistry—distorts the exchange. Because I always listen to you with the mood I'm in, I'm altering your message just as your emotional temperature is altering my message to you. These normal, ever-present emotional highs and lows are uniquely ours. And we listen to everything with this precious uniqueness.

The Replay

I am free of all prejudices. I hate everyone equally.

—W.C. FIELDS

LISTENING SKILL NO. 14
Rate Your Own Listening Skill

The Action

At work or play we interact with many individuals in a given day: spouse, friend, boss, colleague, child. Take a moment to rate how each would perceive *you* as an effective listener on a 1-to-10, low-high scale. Some predictions: (1) your ratings are dissimilar, (2) your friend received a score of 7 or higher, and (3) your boss received a higher rating than your child. You need not be surprised by your ratings, as they are consistent with research findings. We can revise our ratings—that is, if we want to.

The Replay

The average couple spends 12 minutes a day talking to each other; 14 talking to their children—12 of those 14 minutes are devoted to "do this and do that."

—ROSEMARY POTTER

1. INACTIVE • Apathetic • Somnolent • Detached • Drifting • Purposeless • Passive • Uninvolved	**2. REACTIVE** • Defensive • Challenging • Responding • Evocative • Passive/Aggressive • Involved, sometimes reluctantly
3. PROACTIVE • Persistent • Initiating • Provocative • Focused • Demanding • Aggressive/Assertive • Involved, although others may not be	**4. INTERACTIVE** • Aware • Sensitive • Caring • Responsive • Direct • Patient • Assertive • Involved

LISTENING SKILL NO. 15
Note Your Listening Traits

The Action

Four functional sets of listener behaviors can be depicted. Each set embraces certain observable traits (see lists at left).

We employ one of these sets as a basic listening style while another serves as a backup. In practice, of course, we use any one or combination of these traits.

The Replay

A listener is not a special kind of person. Rather, every person is a special kind of listener.

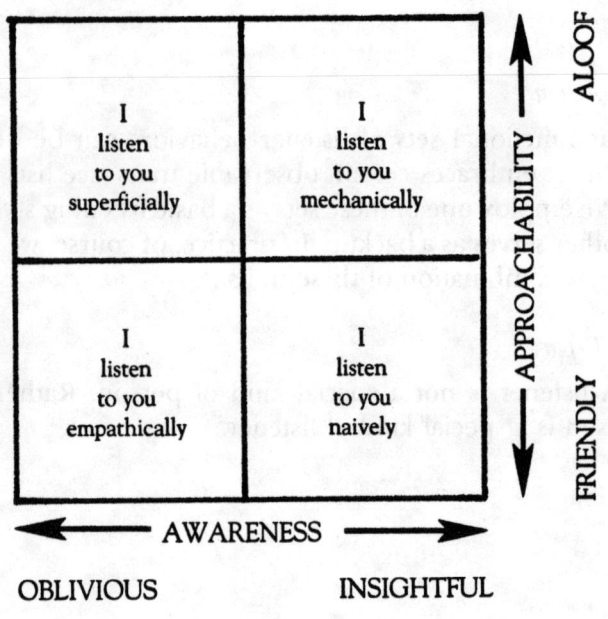

LISTENING SKILL NO. 16
Check Your Patterns

The Action

We listen to each other in degrees of *awareness* (to what extent do I accurately monitor your words, moods, and actions?) and in degrees of *approachability* (to what extent do I allow you to penetrate my outer defenses?). By force-fitting the awareness and approachability factors, we derive four listening patterns (see illustration at left).

Although awareness is a skill and approachability is an attitude, both can be modified to improve listening. Each of us probably follows one of these patterns most of the time and the others some of the time. What's *your* pattern?

The Replay

Manager at staff meeting: My door is always open.
Private reaction by subordinates: True, but *you* aren't!

LISTENING SKILL NO. 17
Respect Your Audience

The Action

We must devote some space to those who give formal presentations to audiences. As listeners we assume that a responsible presenter has something worthwhile to say and knows how to say it effectively. Frequently, however, one or both of these assumptions prove invalid. During a poor presentation, if the boss is watching us, our egress is blocked, our car can't be extracted until the crowd disperses, or we're related to the speaker, then our only recourse is to sit, but not necessarily to suffer. We can mentally decipher what we believe the message to be and speculate on how we would deliver it to a discerning audience like us.

The Replay

Spouse #1: How was your regional meeting today?
Spouse #2: Well, it was all factual stuff, and the presenter read everything to us.
Spouse #1: That's too bad.
Spouse #2: Yeah—besides, he read it badly.
Spouse #1: Why, that's even worse!
Spouse #2: Well, honestly, it didn't matter, since it wasn't worth reading to begin with.
Spouse #1: But he must have said something of value.
Spouse #2: Who knows? I wasn't listening.

LISTENING SKILL NO. 18
Know What You Want

The Action

Certain behaviors virtually guarantee that we will *not* be listened to. Not knowing what we want is one of them. If we want our listener to provide something tangible, to perform an assigned task, or to persuade others to do either, then that listener needs to hear specific information and instructions. If the speaker is uncertain ("I really don't know what I want from you"), confused ("Let me repeat that. I don't think I said what I had intended") or apologetic ("What I'm saying really isn't important"), then the message that the listener will receive is predictable. Uncertainty, confusion, or apology.

The Replay

Ideally, listening is the process of extracting sense from sound. In reality, however, listening is often a process of extracting inexactness.

Size of Group	Multiplier	Number of Potential Exchanges
3	(3-1)	6
10	(10-1)	90
30	(30-1)	870
100	(100-1)	9,900

LISTENING SKILL NO. 19
Count Numbers Because Numbers Count

The Action

"When E. F. Hutton talks, people listen." Substitute *your* name in that sentence. Do people listen? It depends upon who is listening, you say. Yes. The number of listeners is crucial also. Obviously, increasing the number of listeners also increases the amount of possible distortion. Not so obvious, perhaps, is the expanding number of potential exchanges and subsequent misinterpretations as the group size increases. After eliminating self-talk as a consideration, the audience effect is impressive (see table at left).

Since it is important that your listeners concentrate, you need to minimize the potential for distortion. Stopping the action frequently to organize buzz groups or applying other audience participation techniques designed to elicit feedback can improve listening accuracy within larger groups.

The Replay

The number of people in this country who hear is almost nil, slightly more than the number of card-carrying musicians.

—RICHARD BANDLER and JOHN GRINDER
Frogs Into Princes

LISTENING SKILL NO. 20
Regard Old Messages as New Ones

The Action

Another behavior that predictably erodes listening is assuming that we already know what is being said. The resigned "I've heard it all before" automatically disengages the brain, freeing it to forage elsewhere. Since an experience can only be regarded as new when we allow it to be so, we need to refocus our attention. Instead of a "so what else is new" dismissal, we can ask ourselves, "Has he added any ideas?" or "Is what she's saying consistent with what I recall from earlier conversations?" When we listen as though we were hearing a message for the first time, we both focus attention and engage the mind.

The Replay

Heckler at political rally for Al Smith, circa 1928: Tell us everything you know, Al, it won't take very long!
Smith: I'll tell everyone what we *both* know; it won't take any longer!

LISTENING SKILL NO. 21
Listen First, Then Answer

The Action

A friend of mine used to anticipate my words, form them with his lips, and, worse, actually utter my intended message. Sharing a joke was disconcerting. I don't have the fastest drawl in the jest, but he sensed in advance what I was going to say. Although he denied having heard the story, his quick reactions punctured puns before they were airborne. My defense was to invent optional punch lines to detour his retorts. To a lesser degree, we mentally prepare answers before a speaker finishes. Shooting from the lip often misfires because I can't listen to you while I'm talking.

The Replay

The trouble with people who talk too fast is that they often say something they haven't thought about yet.

LISTENING SKILL NO. 22
Don't Blame Your Listener

The Action

Effective communication blends expressive and receptive skills. Knowing that whatever message received *is* the message seems to place the burden of understanding upon the listener. It is the speaker, however, who bears responsibility for the message, takes risks in providing it, and has a wide range of options in delivering it. Whenever I blame my listener for failing to understand me, I ignore my own role in the communication process.

The Replay

If you hear what I want you to hear, then you're a good listener and, obviously, I'm a good explainer.

If you don't hear what I want you to hear, then, obviously, you're a lousy listener.

LISTENING SKILL NO. 23
Respect Listener Differences

The Action

While administering an oral intelligence test, a psychologist asked a 10-year-old Hispanic boy to name the four seasons of the year. He quickly responded, "Salt, pepper, mustard, and ketchup." Assuming the child hadn't heard the question, the psychologist said, "Those are seasonings. Listen again: name the four seasons *of the year.*" Noting the psychologist's emphasis, he replied, "Baseball season, football season, hockey season, and basketball season." Unfortunately, the boy received no credit for his insightful and imaginative answer. Although extracted from a restrictive testing situation, this vignette reminds us to be sensitive to the geographic, linguistic, and ethnic differences among us. Again, what we say is not always what someone else hears.

The Replay

Listening is in the ear of the beholder.

—JOY BLAKE

LISTENING SKILL NO. 24
Listen Carefully

The Action

Are you willing to try a pencil-and-paper listening exercise? Assume that the following directions were provided *orally:*

> *Directions:* "After you hear the word START a second time, read the exercise once and answer the question. Note-taking is permitted. BEGIN."
>
> You're the driver of an empty, parked bus. Seven passengers board. At the first scheduled stop three new passengers board while two leave. At the next stop two passengers leave. Question: How old is the bus driver?

If you wrote anything, you weren't listening. When did you "hear" the word START a second time?

The Replay

For those who weren't listening but did the exercise anyway, *you* were the driver. How old are you? (Incidentally, there were ten passengers, six of whom remained after two stops.)

LISTENING SKILL NO. 25
Listen for Ideas

The Action

Historian Arnold Toynbee once chided his colleagues for placing "facts on the throne and ideas on the scaffold." When there is a choice, effective listeners focus on ideas, since facts can be resurrected. Two important mental functions in listening are recall and comprehension. Recall is a "to have and have not" function involving memory. It is that portion of what we hear that can be restated later. Comprehension is a "to have and to hold" function involving mastery. It is the portion of what we hear that is thoroughly understood and intelligently applied. While I may have a vast memory without mastery, I cannot have mastery without memory. Let the ideas rule without hanging the facts.

The Replay

Good listeners think more broadly—because they hear and understand more facts and points of view. Because listeners look at problems with fresh eyes, combine what they learn in more unlikely ways, they're more apt to hit upon truly startling ideas.

—A Sperry Advertisement

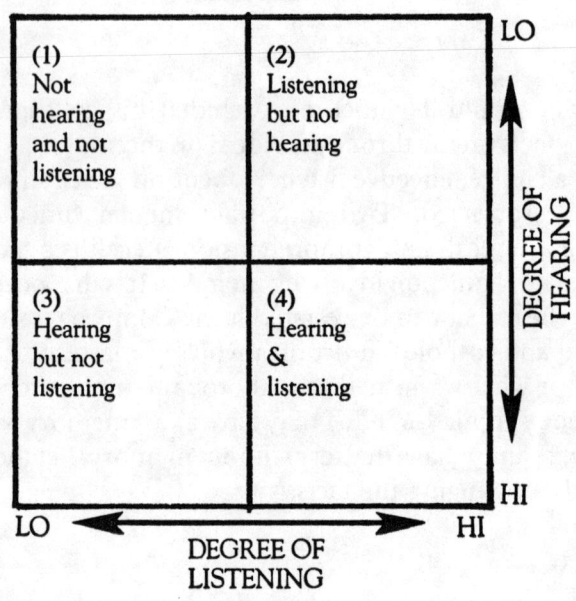

LISTENING SKILL NO. 26
Acknowledge the Consequences of Not Listening

The Action

The force-fit of listening skill and auditory receptivity creates four possible conditions: (1) not hearing and not listening, (2) listening but not hearing, (3) hearing but not listening, and (4) hearing and listening (see illustration at left).

The first condition, a near-comatose state, suggests ignorance and apathy. In the second condition, only partial messages are received since we must rely on an array of often unreliable visual cues. The third condition guarantees wrong turns, missed data, and the possible erosion of relationships. The fourth condition offers an opportunity for empathy, understanding, and acceptance. It pays to hear *and* to listen.

The Replay

Danny: What's the difference between ignorance and apathy?
Joe: I don't know and I don't care!
Zack: Like I always say, ask a dumb question and you get a dumb answer.

LISTENING SKILL NO. 27
Listen Smarter

The Action

Although we have stressed the importance of listening for ideas, we don't want to shortchange factual material. A common problem is how to gather the facts from a rapid-fire delivery. Our listening ability draws blanks as we shield ourselves from frustration or panic. While we're probably not equipped to listen both faster and better, we can listen smarter. Before being inundated by a "data banker," we can ask: Do I need to hear this? If not, can someone else sit in who does? How much do I need to know? Is this material written down? Is it available? Can the material be taped for later replay and study? Can we schedule frequent breaks to relax and review the material in smaller doses? Smart listeners listen smart.

The Replay

He could charm an audience an hour on a stretch without ever getting rid of an idea.

—MARK TWAIN

LISTENING SKILL NO. 28
Listen Silently

The Action

Ironically, the silent skill of listening relies upon sound. Rearranging the letters L-I-S-T-E-N produces S-I-L-E-N-T. When we're silent, attentive, and receptive, a special kind of listening is possible. Psychoanalyst Theodore Reik called this "listening with the third ear." Our internal listening ear mulls, interprets, speculates, posits, and reviews. The active listener tunes in to the speaker's non-verbal gestures, subtle meanings, inner feelings, and unstated messages.

The Replay

I know that you're really listening to me when you hear what I'm *not* saying.

LISTENING SKILL NO. 29
Interpret Paralanguage

The Action

When we utter sounds without words, we are using paralanguage. Grins and grimaces are forms of body language; grunts and groans are paralanguage. Occasionally, as in a yawn, the categories overlap. A noisy yawn is paralanguage; a silent one is not. But both are examples of body language. Though the sounds lack words, they don't lack purpose or meaning. We use "oh?" and "hmmm," for example, to signal interest and to elicit response. "Ugh" and "yecch" are paralanguage for dislike. We can further increase our listening quotient by learning to interpret the various tones of grunts and groans. (Huh?)

The Replay

Lion #1: Why did you devour the friendly anthropologist? You know all of us enjoyed listening to his classical records. How could you be so insensitive?

Lion #2: EHHH?

LISTENING SKILL NO. 30
Respect Attention Spans

The Action

Attention span—the sheer amount of time we willingly devote to an activity—varies with our personal interests, priorities, energy level, and time availability. A sensitive speaker introduced late in a seemingly endless program often elicits cheers of relief or respect when he voluntarily shreds his notes and bids his audience a good wish and a good night. Because the mind can absorb only what the seat can endure, most of us have a short tolerance for long-windedness. If all of us would respect this adage, none of us would ever endure the pain of verbal overkill.

The Replay

Long-winded speaker: I seem to have lost track of the time. Does anyone have a watch?

Short-fused listener: No, but there's a calendar hanging on the wall behind you!

LISTENING SKILL NO. 31
Include Us All in Conversation

The Action

Those who write about communication processes disagree on how many "persons" are included in a single dialogue. Two, four, six, or eight—how many communicate? Let's try six: what you and I intend to say (two), what each of us actually says (two), and what each of us believes we heard (two). Admittedly, tracking all of the "voices" in a single two-party conversation is difficult. This array of messages can either deter effective listening or provide an opportunity for achieving it. Both the choice and the challenge are ever-present.

The Replay

I know that you think you heard what I said, but is what you heard what I really meant?

LISTENING SKILL NO. 32
Repeat What You Hear

The Action

We usually assume that a message sent is a message received. When a listener repeats aloud important facts, directions, or ideas that we have provided, our assumptions are either confirmed or denied. While we may not know immediately if our listener will retain the information, revise it, react to it, or reject it, we do know that he or she did at least *receive* it. Likewise, when we repeat or rephrase messages for our listeners, we improve, if not guarantee, the quality of our conversations.

The Replay

Steve Martin:	Let's repeat the Non-Conformists' Oath: I promise to be different!
Audience:	I promise to be different!
Martin:	I promise to be unique!
Audience:	I promise to be unique!
Martin:	I promise not to repeat things other people say!
Audience:	I promise not to . . .

LISTENING SKILL NO. 33
Guard Against Drifting

The Action

Dispositionally, everyone has a right to be someplace. At any one time the "right" place could be a disposition to unite, to fight, toward fright or flight. A "flight" disposition can adversely affect listening. If in conversation we're mentally in outer spaces, acting in alternate places, or interacting with other faces, then listening suffers. Such aimless drifting causes messages to be missed. We can rejoin our inner conversations later, but we can't relive the reality called now. We must put the there-and-then on hold and hold on to the here-and-now. To do otherwise is to help create an illusion that we have communicated when, in fact, we have not.

The Replay

Manager: I don't believe you heard what I said!
Supervisor: I heard what you said; I just wasn't listening.

LISTENING SKILL NO. 34
Mind Your Manner

The Action

The manner in which you make a request profoundly affects your listener's behavior. Requests range in *frequency* from non-stop commands to putting all your begs in one "ask-it." Requests range in *intensity* from a drowsy "wake me when it's over" to a frantic "watch out, we're going to crash!" Requests also range in *manner:* a suggestive ad—"Fly now, pay later"; an unspoken wish—"Play it again, Sam"; a predictable command—"Book 'em, Dano; murder one"; an evasive action—"Let George do it"; an informal order—"Hey Mabel, Black Label." While frequency and intensity are important factors influencing listener behavior, the actual and perceived manner of a request involves the listener in more subtle and, sometimes, more permanent ways.

The Replay

There is only one manner of hearing but many manners of listening.

SPATIAL DIMENSION	PREFERRED DISTANCE	AUDIENCE	LOCALE	VOLUME
Intimate	0-2'	Family, lovers	Inner, private spaces	Quiet talk, whispers
Interpersonal	2-3'	Friends, colleagues	Offices, restaurants	Normal volume & pitch
Impersonal	3-8'	Foreigners, strangers	Sidewalks, stores	Sufficient volume to offset background noise
Infinite	8' to Infinity	Anyone tuned into frequency	Outer, unknown spaces	Appropriate amplification from smoke signals to atomic blasts

LISTENING SKILL NO. 35
Select Your Listening Space

The Action

Each of us has a comfort zone in which we maintain a preferred and predictable distance from those with whom we interact. The comfort zone variables include familiarity, distance, location, and ethnic origin. The four basic American patterns or listening posts are called *Intimate, Interpersonal, Impersonal,* and *Infinite* (see table at left).

Listening space is largely determined not by who we know, but rather how well we know one another or how much we really want to know one another.

The Replay

Old principle of communication: Close and frequent contact between people guarantees good listening.

New interpretation of old principle of communication: If that's true, why do nearly half of all American marriages end in divorce?

MESSAGES WITHIN WORK SETTINGS	% THOUGHTS	% FEELINGS
Normal Balance in Messages	50	50
Frequency of Expression	90	10
Intensity of Expression	10	90

LISTENING SKILL NO. 36
Listen for Feelings and Reduce Costs

The Action

In work settings it is not uncommon for feelings to be suppressed. "You're supposed to *think* around here" is the working norm; "I'm not here to deal with people's feelings" is the managerial attitude. Because messages are part thought and part feeling, it's costly to *not* listen on both frequencies (see table at left).

Note that all of that "heavy" thinking we do carries a very low intensity, yet our feelings, once expressed, carry a frighteningly high level of intensity. Holding feelings in check in fear or by choice is counterproductive. Although there is some risk involved in ignoring feelings and failing to hear, there is also a high cost to individuals and to their organizations.

The Replay

Too caustic? To hell with the cost, we'll make the picture anyway.

—SAMUEL GOLDWYN

LISTENING SKILL NO. 37
Unclutter Your Speech

The Action

Once, during an uneventful group meeting, I recorded tally marks for each "you know" that one of my colleagues uttered. After he finished, I passed him a note that read, "I don't recall what you said, but you used the phrase 'you know' forty-three times in less than four minutes!" Much later he thanked me, you know, for what I had, you know, done. Cluttered speech distorts messages. To avoid the loss of either messages or friends, we need to limit our use of meaningless expressions. If a best friend won't help, perhaps a self-check will. Well, uh, you know, uh, am I cluttering, uh, my own speech? Uh, you know, you know what I mean?

The Replay

The law of the verbal detour: Well, uh, in some conversations the shortest distance between, uh, two points is, you know, always, uh, under construction.

LISTENING SKILL NO. 38
See More, Hear More

The Action

In conversations, I need eye contact to hear well. When you avoid eye contact with me or look at me directly through dark glasses, I don't hear very well. And if you are wearing mirrored sunglasses, your message will be virtually inaudible to me as I "listen" to my image in your lenses. Part of my dilemma, of course, results from missing some vital visual cues. More important, however, is my impression that wandering or evasive eyes signal a lack of interest or even a lack of truthfulness. I realize that these observations are invalid. It's more or less a cultural phenomenon. There are individuals throughout the world who are conditioned in various ways to avoid direct eye contact. Well, it's my problem and I'm working on it. Meanwhile, would you please remove your sunglasses?

The Replay

Perhaps it's actually "hear more, see more." For if I didn't have two ears, how could I keep my glasses on?

LISTENING SKILL NO. 39
Say More, Hear More

The Action

What we say influences what we hear. Calvin Coolidge advocated silence: "You don't have to explain something you haven't said." Unfortunately, silence yields more rust than gold. A what-I-don't-say-can't-hurt-me attitude erodes most exchanges. My reticence can convey unawareness, disinterest, or an unwillingness to share information. The likely consequence is that you will also say less. Whenever I withdraw for whatever reason, I discourage an open and honest dialogue.

The Replay

Don't talk unless you can improve the silence.

LISTENING SKILL NO. 40
Consider the Arena

The Action

Where we view an event affects what we see and hear. Note the environmental differences between being scrunched by 10,000 basketball fans in a 9,500-capacity gym and being scattered among 10,000 baseball fans in a 50,000-capacity stadium. This arena effect impacts upon our need for personal space, the amount of distraction, decibel levels, intensity of involvement, concern for safety and, of course, our ability to listen. Companions form groups, groups can become crowds and, occasionally, crowds erupt into mobs. As the degree of compactness increases, we hear more and listen less. The dissonance makes a difference.

The Replay

A ten-year-old boy from San Juan visited New York with a heartfelt wish to see the Yankees play. A persuasive uncle secured the very last seat in an oversold stadium—atop the center field flagpole. The post-game conversation:

Uncle: Did you enjoy the game?
José: Yes, and everyone was so considerate!
Uncle: What do you mean?
José: Well, the people wanted to know if my seat was okay. Just before the game, everyone stood up, faced me, and shouted, "José, can you see?"

LISTENING SKILL NO. 41
Engage Your Listener Gently

The Action

During my brief military obligation I always froze at two shrill commands: "Now hear this!" and "Listen up!" Never once did I hear the polite and plaintive "May I have your attention, please?" Well, it worked. Partially. Shrillness did elicit an unwavering stillness. But somehow the messages, amplified via a leather-lunged drill instructor, usually provoked a "what was that all about?" or a "what did he say?" This approach fixes attention but paralyzes the brain. One cannot command another to listen.

The Replay

Whisper in my ear and I'll follow you anywhere.

LISTENING SKILL NO. 42
Avoid Compulsive Talkers

The Action

Everyone can contribute something to an organization. One can always serve as a bad example. Even compulsive talkers contribute something: they teach us not to listen. Endless diatribe is the number-one deterrent to effective listening. If one has nothing to say and keeps on talking, what's to be gained? Anything times nothing always equals nothing. Since most of us decline to challenge compulsive talkers, we resort to other devices: avoidance, non-listening, or (in extreme cases) strangulation. We sometimes *pretend* to listen, thereby encouraging the compulsive talker. Pretending to listen is hard work, so who's the troubled one? My run-off-at-the-mouth acquaintance, or me, the singed-ear masochist?

The Replay

People have to talk about something just to keep their voice boxes in working order so they'll have good boxes in case there's ever anything really meaningful to say.

—KURT VONNEGUT, JR.

LISTENING SKILL NO. 43
Question Unclear Signals

The Action

Every once in a while we see signs that unintentionally confuse and amuse us. A current favorite in a Boston restaurant warns customers, "This is an emergency exit. Do not use under any circumstances." We read, smile, and ignore. Failure to clarify can be fatal. Recall the rancher screaming to the hired hand, "*Shod,* you dummy! I wanted the horse *shod,* not *shot!*" We tend not to stop and question those who deliver confusing spoken signals, because we are afraid to embarrass the speaker or determined not to reveal our own inability to understand. So when in doubt, doubt. Hear not, heed not.

The Replay

The first-photocopy story: Executive with newly installed photocopying equipment gives an original document, the only one in existence, to an assistant with the instruction, "Burn it!" The assistant did. With a match.

LISTENING SKILL NO. 44
Listen for Meaning

The Action

Let's examine the thought part of a message. What exactly does the speaker want? For example, an experienced reservations clerk for a popular resort motel might hear the following requests on a given day:

Request	Possible Interpretation
"I want two twin beds"	"Does the party really want *four* beds?"
"I want a single double"	"Let's see, that's one room, two people?"
"I want two singles"	"Is that rooms or beds?"
"I want a double single"	"Oh, you want one room with a double bed? Or maybe two single rooms?"
"I want adjoining rooms with a door between."	"Adjoining rooms don't have doors between them. You want *connecting* rooms?"

Again, it isn't quite cricket to blame the speaker because we hear something unclearly. It's up to us to listen *and* to elicit the real meaning. Sometimes it requires quite an imagination.

The Replay

Motel clerk: What type of accommodation would you prefer, sir?

Tourist: Down-and-out, poolside.

Clerk: Sir, we can give you up-and-in and down-and-in poolside or, if you prefer, up-and-out and down-and-out roadside, but you can't be down, out, and in at the same time!

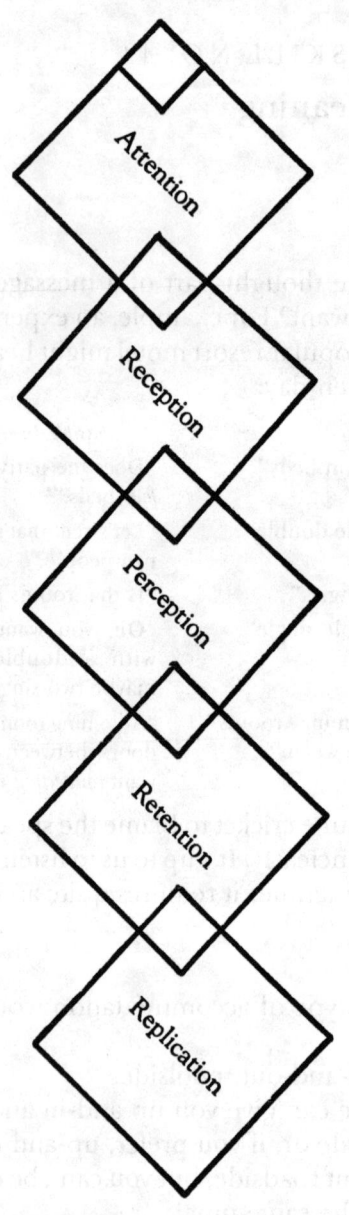

LISTENING SKILL NO. 45
Listen to Know

The Action

We are endowed with remarkably intricate sensory equipment that permits us to monitor our environment efficiently. The sights, sounds, smells, and strokes of our external world provide the raw data for internal processing. As external stimuli merge into infinite patterns, internal functions are miraculously linked to them. A simple model for listening can be depicted (see illustration at left).

Listening converts sensory sounds into soundless sense.

The Replay

If I don't know I don't know, I think I know.
If I don't know I know, I think I don't know.

—R. D. LAING

LISTENING SKILL NO. 46
Listen Carefully to Your Tapes

The Action

According to psychologist Albert Ellis, we often invite unnecessary personal trauma when we react to our own exaggerated interpretations of what we have heard rather than to what we actually hear. An unintentional work-related mistake verbally noted by the boss, for example, can evoke such internal, amplified self-criticism as "she must think I'm an idiot," "I'm unworthy of the trust she's given me," or "I'm going to hear about this again during my next evaluation." When we freely and openly acknowledge such errors and resolve not to repeat them, we clear the way for productive effort. When we listen to our own exaggerated messages of gloom and doom, we can become temporarily immobilized. What we hear is seldom as destructive as our own internally taped replay.

The Replay

   Is it me or is it Memorex?

LISTENING SKILL NO. 47
Reduce the Signals

The Action

When the owners of professional sports teams extended their schedules, they created overlapping seasons, forcing them to compete for our attention. During one such period, I watched a sports fanatic masterfully track two television games and one radio game simultaneously, without confusing each game's fouls, penalties, errors, or commercials. He had learned to mix the sights of slam dunks and body checks with the sounds of base hits and pitched beers into a comprehensible collage of sensory data. Political legend has it that a former occupant of the White House could watch and comprehend simultaneous ABC, CBS, and NBC news telecasts in the same way. While most of us cannot extract meaning from such a babble of sounds, we can sort out what we want to hear while allowing other sounds to reverberate unattended. If given a choice, we play attention to only one game at a time.

The Replay

A ballpark exchange:
Fan #1: How can you watch this game while you're wired to your radio listening to another game?
Fan #2: I'm listening to *this* game. I like to hear what I'm seeing.

LISTENING SKILL NO. 48
Avoid Noise Pollution When You Can

The Action

Defining noise as unwanted sound creates an interesting paradox, since anything producing sound causes distortion in what we hear and think. We're not addressing work-related, chronic noise here—the kind that induces occupational deafness—but, rather, the more subtle, individually controlled noise pollutants near our work and play areas. The rhythms from your stereo may be music to your ears but noise to mine. Researchers suggest that environmental noise invades our comfort zone and produces attendant psychological reactions ranging from irritability to sexual impotence. Since my psyche doesn't need such excessive static, can we continue this conversation later, elsewhere? Say, at your place?

The Replay

Sergeant to gun crew after 600 rounds of heavy artillery had been dumped upon the enemy: "Shhh, quiet down! Do you want them to know where we are?"

LISTENING SKILL NO. 49

Reduce Noise Pollution When You Can't Avoid It

The Action

Q: Why are you hitting your head against the wall?
A: Because it feels so good when I stop!
Q: What will you do when you break into the next room?
A: By then I won't need an answer.

So it is with gradual hearing loss caused by excessive and frequent environmental noise. Although we converse within a 45-75 decibel (dB) range, the upper level of this range is considered loud, and a 100-decibel level is potentially harmful. (Other examples: nearby phone ringing—75 dB; food blender—90 dB; rock band—115 dB; pain threshold—130 dB.) Periodic sound-level meter readings in factories, offices, schools and homes can point out conditions that may cause gradual noise-induced hearing losses. Reducing noise pollutants enables us to hear better and longer—and it feels so good when the plugs are pulled.

The Replay

A radio station surveyed rock musicians to determine the possible effects of long-term high-decibel sound on hearing loss. The findings:

40 percent of those surveyed shouted, "No loss!"
60 percent didn't hear the question.

LISTENING SKILL NO. 50
When You Can't Hear, Say So

The Action

We occasionally continue the pretense of conversing when we cannot "hear" the other person. Regional accents or dialects, speech patterns, soft voices, and environmental noise are contributing factors. Rather than ask our companion to repeat, speak up, slow down, or move to a quieter space, we nod, smile, maintain eye contact, and utter an assenting "yes" or "uh huh." Perhaps it's not a case of not wanting to listen but one of not wanting to embarrass our companion. Or, possibly, our reticence comes from *our* not wanting to be embarrassed. Either way, messages are mixed and friendships are fractured.

The Replay

She: You haven't heard a word I've said!
He: Did you say something?

LISTENING SKILL NO. 51
Case the Space

The Action

The flip side of limited hearing caused by environmental noise is the ability to focus upon meaningful messages amid a cacophony of sound. We call this the Cocktail Party Phenomenon. Simultaneous conversations fill a crowded space, but we are somehow able to pick up distinct messages from a distant source, despite the intervening clusters of chatter. While we nod, smile, and appear to converse with those nearby, we're savoring another group's conversation at a distance. This use of our "antennae" can also be disconcerting—we can never be certain who's listening to *us*.

The Replay

Eavesdrop—Something to do when what you're supposed to hear isn't worth listening to, and what you're not supposed to hear *is*.

MEDIUM	PRIMARY SOURCES OF SENSORY DATA	DIRECTIONAL FLOW OF COMMUNICATION	LEVEL OF MESSAGE ACCEPTANCE/REJECTION	USUAL LEVEL OF LISTENER RETENTION	USUAL LEVEL OF LISTENER INVOLVEMENT
RADIO	Voice, music, and other sounds	Predominantly one-way	Relatively unknown	Low 1	Low 1
TELEPHONE	Voice, transmission noise & some environmental sound	Usually two-way	Relatively known	2	2
TELEVISION	Voice, other sounds, and arbitrarily focused visual cues	Predominantly one-way	Relatively unknown	3	3
FACE-TO-FACE	Voice, focused visual cues, touch, smell, environmental sound	Usually two-way	Usually known	4	4
SELF-TALK	Stored external sensory data plus internal emotional state	Normally one-way	Ultimately known	5 High	5 High

LISTENING SKILL NO. 52
Match the Message with the Medium

The Action

We can glean two important observations from the summary table shown: (1) two-way communication is usually—but not always—more effective than one-way communication, and (2) visual images are more involving than auditory messages are (see table at left).

Self-talk, where the individual *is* the only active participant, is based upon stored experience-based data—things we've heard, seen, touched, smelled—and the individual's emotional state at the moment.

The Replay

It's not what you hear, it's how and where you hear it.

LISTENING SKILL NO. 53
Know When to Talk

The Action

We've previously emphasized the value of silence to empathic listening. An extension of this skill is knowing *when* to be silent. As Jonathan Swift says in *Gulliver's Travels,* "There are times when talk is hurtful and when silence is the beginning of wisdom. Do you know when?" Knowing when is a personal challenge for us. If listening is enriching, then talking must be limiting. Once again, more is less because I can't listen when I'm doing all of the talking.

The Replay

#311—If you talk, you repeat what you already know. If you listen you learn.

#766—He who talks incessantly, talks nonsense.

—Hsing Ling Fortune Cookies

LISTENING SKILL NO. 54
Provide Specific Information

The Action

The less specific we are, the harder our listener has to work. Examine the following exchange between two friends:

#1: I just bought a car.
#2: New?
#1: Used.
#2: Domestic?
#1: Foreign.
#2: German?
#1: Japanese.
#2: Toyota?
#1: Datsun!

How much easier it would have been for the listener if the speaker had opened with, "I just bought a used Datsun."

The Replay

Japanese auto producer:	We must find a name for our latest export model—and *fast!*
Advertising executive:	How much time do we have?
Producer:	I need it by noon today!
Adman:	Datsun?

LISTENING SKILL NO. 55
Indulge the Diverters

The Action

Some listeners have a disconcerting ability to redirect or divert messages. Apparently, these diverters learn their craft early and sharpen it throughout life. For example, when one youngster received his first zero in school, his defensive reply to his parents' "What happened?" query was, "The teacher ran out of stars and gave me a moon." A math major, asked by his grandmother to "say something in mathematics," replied "πr^2"—whereupon the older woman protested, "Now, everybody know that pie are *round*. *Cornbread* are square!" The kindest way to deal with such listeners is to savor their inventiveness and start again at square one—even if, as in these illustrations, the square is round.

The Replay

Virginia farmer: Just how big is your spread?
Texas rancher: Well, if I get in my truck at sunup and drive all day, I'm still on my land at sundown.
Virginia farmer: Yeah, I had a truck like that once too!

LISTENING SKILL NO. 56
Hear Ye! The Eyes Have It

The Action

Our principal sensory receptors process data gathered from sight, sound, and bodily movement. Proponents of one emerging communications model claim that most of us are "wired together" quite consistently, and that a process called eye watching can reveal cues indicating a person's principal sensory receptor. The eye movements of a hearing-oriented processor, for example, are often from side to side, indicating that this person is making immediate sense of sounds. By feeding this auditory learner messages such as "I really *tune in* to you," "it *sounds* okay," or "let's give him a *ring,*" we activate his appropriate receptors, conveying to him our own heightened awareness and sensitivity.

The Replay

While your voice shapes one message, your eyes share another. And although I hear your words, I listen to your eyes.

LISTENING SKILL NO. 57
Be at Ease with Those Wearing Bright Feathers

The Action

Power, size, rank, and status affect how we listen. Isn't the "chief" within any organization, for example, given special attentiveness? After all, the basic rules of management are: (1) the boss is the boss; and (2) if you have any doubt as to who the boss is, re-read Rule 1. Certain people actually immobilize us. I still recall a liberty shortly after marine boot camp when, awed by a USMC colonel displaying an array of eagles, wings, ribbons, and battle stars, I yielded a clumsy, clammy salute. It was John Wayne on location. All he said was "At ease, son"— which *is* the appropriate message for those similarly awed.

The Replay

She: I own a 500-lb. parrot.
He: Oh? What does it say?
She: Anything it wants.

LISTENING SKILL NO. 58
Insist Upon Two-Way Exchanges

The Action

There is an effective way to illustrate the difference between one- and two-way communication. A person facing away from a group describes the drawing of connecting rectangles shown here. The group members, told to remain silent, are asked to reproduce the unseen drawing.

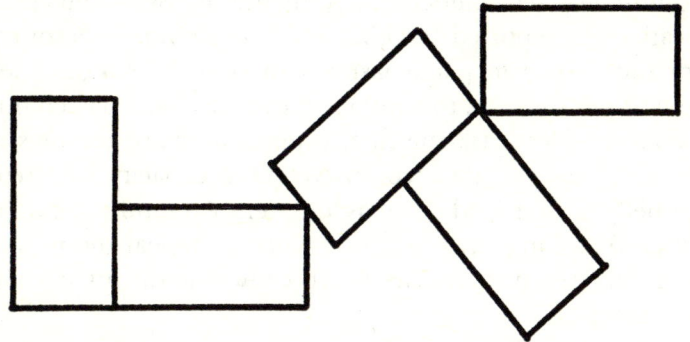

Predictably, participants listening to what seem to be conflicting instructions given without the aid of body language cues soon become frustrated or bored. When the exercise is repeated with the speaker facing the group and describing a new configuration, and with group members now permitted to ask questions, both interest and accuracy dramatically improve. The essential distinction, then, is that in two-way communication, listeners have an opportunity to clarify the messages they receive.

The Replay

Unless you tell me what you're hearing, I can't be certain of what I'm actually saying.

LISTENING SKILL NO. 59
Beware of Distortions

The Action

According to mathematician Norbert Weiner, "Speech is a joint game between talker and listener against the forces of confusion." Here's an activity to prove his point. Before a quiet social gathering of a dozen or so friends, mentally prepare a brief news item such as, "A private plane and a commercial jet collided today in the air over France. No deaths were reported, but nine jet passengers are unaccounted for and the private plane hasn't been located." Ask one friend to whisper the item to another until it has been passed on to everyone. Now, ask the final listener to share the message openly. Are the data confused? Our capacity to stretch, embellish, alter, and delete is apparently boundless. End the game by asking each person in turn to repeat the message originally received. At least you'll know who distorted what—this time.

The Replay

Father to young son: I've told you sixty million times not to exaggerate!

LISTENING SKILL NO. 60
Muzzle Those Who Roar

The Action

A popular detergent commercial shrieks, "Shout it out!" What works for grime-lifting makes for grim listening. High-volume life-or-death entreaties, histrionic fits, or strident commentary upset the natural serenity for most people—except those who, let's say, prefer awakening to a raucous rooster or a clanging clock instead of a soothing serenade. Well, I say farewell to alarmists. I somehow listen better to less-emotional pitches. Anyone for tea and symphony?

The Replay

"I'll never pet that lion again!" he said offhandedly.

LISTENING SKILL NO. 61
Listen—If at First You Don't Heed, Hear Again

The Action

Whether it's learning to cipher, emptying the trash, or following advice, we tend to perform to others' expectations only when we're ready and willing. Advice-giving illustrates the point. Parents, preachers, and psychiatrists have long noted that progeny, parishioners, and patients accept what they hear only when they are ready and willing to hear what they hear. This experience of "seeing the light" often takes place hours, days, months, or even years later. Thus, we have another hearing phenomenon: delayed listening. We say to ourselves, "*Now* I know what she meant" or "He's been trying to tell me that for some time." Physics to the contrary, light can sometimes travel slower than sound.

The Replay

Replays are not always instant.

LISTENING SKILL NO. 62
Interrupt Whenever Necessary

The Action

When we were very young, we were told never to interrupt others while they were talking. The "others," of course, were our parents and various authority figures. Such programming effectively controlled our natural interruptive impulses. As adults, we've unnecessarily retained this conditioned silence. However, certain situations actually invite interruptions: danger, not hearing, not understanding, misunderstanding, misstatement, too-familiar jokes and previously shared details of surgery. During these interactions we have a responsibility to interrupt, since matters of safety, savvy, or sanity are involved. At other times, an interruption remains an annoyance.

The Replay

The bathtub was invented in 1850. The telephone was invented in 1875. Just imagine, people living in 1850 could have relaxed in their bathtubs for twenty-five years without being interrupted by the phone ringing.

LISTENING SKILL NO. 63
Remember the Pain

The Action

The quality of previous interactions between two persons is an important factor in determining how productively each listens to the other. If their prior exchanges were cordial, comfortable, and considerate, this kind of behavior is likely to characterize their next conversation as well. However, when bickering, bantering, and badgering form the legacy, beware. Lacking thorns and talons, we use words both to protect and to provoke. How one inflicts the pain now becomes the game of the name.

The Replay

Film star #1: I enjoyed your autobiography. Who wrote it for you?
Film star #2: I'm glad you enjoyed it. Who read it to you?

LISTENING SKILL NO. 64
Deflate the Flatulent

The Action

Occasionally, we encounter a kind of person who is very difficult to listen to: the self-styled paragon of verbal perfection. This modern-day oracle has the "correct" answer for whatever question is asked, along with unsolicited commentary about other issues. The challenge, of course, is to maintain a level of listening that will allow us to extract needed information while ignoring the disquieting know-it-all arrogance. According to a well-known story, a young sports reporter once tackled an entire group of know-it-alls: the veteran sportswriters, ex-athletes all, who seriously questioned the credentials of the rookie recently assigned to work with them. They decried the newcomer's lack of letters and trophies and his absence of on-the-field athletic experience. The young reporter's now classic rejoinder: "Before being reassigned I wrote obituary notices, and I didn't have to die to do *them!*"

The Replay

I'm often wrong, but never in doubt.

—BILLY PACKER
TV sports analyst

LISTENING SKILL NO. 65
Try Mnemonics

The Action

Our forgetting curves usually display two consistent characteristics—sharp and upward. Names and numbers, dates and places elude recall. The primary cause is inattentiveness. "Did he say turn right or turn left?" "Was the dosage three pills twice daily or vice versa?" "Let's see, her name was Ginny May, or was it Minnie Gay?" Those who specialize in helping others recall details suggest that we practice various forms of associative memory skills. Rhyming names with familiar or outlandish objects, following patterns to put events in sequence, and forming initial letters into key words are among these "coathook" techniques that hang personal meaning onto elusive facts.

The Replay

ROY G. BIV—associative technique for remembering the colors of the spectrum in sequence: Red, Orange, Yellow, Green, Blue, Indigo, Violet.

LISTENING SKILL NO. 66
Listen to Those Who Know

The Action

The difference between basic and applied researchers is that the former fishes in a pond, while the latter fishes in a pond where there are known to be fish. Similarly, to get the most accurate information we can, we seek, whenever possible, a person known to be knowledgeable. We're understandably wary when we hear any response that begins with "I believe," "It seems as if," "They might," "If I recall," "I'm not sure, but," or "I'm almost absolutely certain." Listening to and acting upon what follows such phrases may leave us upstream without a paddle, downstream in the rapids, or conducting basic research instead of catching fish.

The Replay

Novice fisherman #1
in rented rowboat: Wow! Mark the spot where we hauled in *that* one!
Novice fisherman #2: Right!
#1 (later, ashore): Did you mark the spot?
#2: Sure did. Right on the side of the boat where we landed the big one.
#1: You dummy! We probably won't get the same boat next time!

LISTENING SKILL NO. 67
Hear Not, Heed Not

The Action

How many times have you asked the question "Did you hear what I said?" Countless times, you say? I'll wager you received a one-word response usually beginning with the letter *y*—"yes," "yep," "yup," or that strange utterance "yo." And then what happened? That's right; everything continued as before. That is, before whatever was said, was said and whatever was supposedly heard, was heard. After all, who wants to confess to *not* listening? It's simpler to pretend you didn't ask "Did you hear what I said?" Now, if you *really* want an answer, change the question to "What did you hear?"

The Replay

Q: Didn't I tell you to pay attention?
A: I don't know. I didn't hear what you said.

LISTENING SKILL NO. 68
Be Wary of Extended Silences

The Action

Most of us converse easily and often to sustain workable relationships. In paired exchanges, if one partner or colleague engages in frequent or extended silences, it forces the other to become a mind- and body-reader. An intentional silence in place of a sharing of information can easily change a penny-for-your-thoughts overture to an I-really-don't-give-two-cents-for-your-opinion-anyway posture. Thus, the so-called golden standard of silence impales its bearer.

The Replay

He: For God's sake, say something!
She: Something.

LISTENING SKILL NO. 69
Digest the Dry and the Difficult

The Action

Medieval scholars regarded the brain as a muscle. Modern researchers define the brain as a storage vehicle for electrochemical impulses. Yesterday's alchemists and today's neurobiologists agree, however, on one aspect of brain functioning: "Use it or lose it!" Unfortunately, we tend to tune out dry or difficult subjects. After all, a talk describing the metaphysics of pragmatism isn't likely to draw a large audience. But ethereal or esoteric topics can:
1. Extend our understanding ("I didn't know that . . .")
2. Expand our attitudes ("I feel differently about . . .")
3. Exercise our skills ("I'm now able to . . .")

Energizing the brain, if only occasionally, by listening to challenging material enables our between-the-ears computer to function. Tune-ups are better than tune-outs.

The Replay

To collect sets in your mind is easy, but to decipher a pattern is difficult.

—EDWARD T. HALL
The Silent Language

LISTENING SKILL NO. 70
Beware of Lionizing Body Language

The Action

Despite dire warnings, a young African missionary took a long walk in lion territory. He encountered a ferocious, hungry lion. Since he was unable to outrun the beast, was carrying no firearms, and had no trees to climb, the missionary's options were limited. He knelt, resorting to his first line of defense: prayer. After several unmolested moments of fervent pleading toward Heaven, he tilted his head, opened one eye, and looked at the lion. To his surprise, the beast was crouching close by as if he, too, were praying. The missionary jumped to his feet and exclaimed, "Thank you, Mr. Lion, for sparing my life!" The lion in like fashion tilted his head, opened one eye and roared, "Shut up! I'm saying the blessing."

The Replay

Pray now and prey later.

LISTENING SKILL NO. 71

Acknowledge the Distinction Between the Medium and the Message

The Action

The telegraph, the phonograph, and the telephone replaced distant drums, cave drawings, and smoke signals as means of recording and transmitting information. Silicon chips and magnetic strips, however, only indicate our sophistication in the *technical* aspects of communication. Although our methods of receiving, recording, and retrieving data are more precise now, human understanding and acceptance remain imprecise. It seems the closer we approach Marshall McLuhan's "global village," the more distant the inhabitants are. Can we send drum messages via satellite?

The Replay

First words:

Telegraph: "What hath God wrought?"—Samuel F. B. Morse
Recorder: "Mary had a little lamb."—Thomas A. Edison
Telephone: "Mr. Watson, come here, I want you."
—Alexander Graham Bell

LISTENING SKILL NO. 72
Reduce the Effort, Increase the Reward

The Action

Wilbur Schramm's fraction of selection—the relationship of reward to effort—can be applied to listening:

$$\frac{\text{EXPECTATION OF REWARD (+)}}{\text{EFFORT REQUIRED (−)}}$$

We can enhance another's skill in listening by reducing the *effort required* for our listener (by being clear and precise, encouraging feedback, and reducing distractions) and by increasing the *expectation of reward* for our listener (by being certain that any and all of the listener's what's-in-this-for-me questions are addressed). Two words that regularly appear on lists of "the ten most powerful words" are *free* and *benefit*. By making my message as dissonance-*free* as possible, and by clarifying whatever *benefit* my message has for you, I'll help you listen more effectively to me.

The Replay

A short course in improving someone else's listening skills:

The six most important words:	"I admit I made a mistake."
The five most important words:	"You did a good job."
The four most important words:	"What is your opinion?"
The three most important words:	"If you please."
The two most important words:	"Thank you."
The one most important word:	"We"

LISTENING SKILL NO. 73
Avoid Heavy Winds and Dense Fog

The Action

We assist listeners by using words to express rather than to impress. Messages that are heavily laden with "bafflegab"—a fog-shrouded assortment of old-fashioned, unclear, inflated, or invented verbal static—ensure faulty reception. Spokespersons for large bureaucratic enterprises seem to be particularly fond of uttering simple thoughts cleverly disguised as complex clouds. Briefings become drenchings. Whenever we change a clear breeze to a heavy wind, we punish our listener, who predictably retaliates with inattention and future avoidance. Sound doesn't carry well through dense fog. But on a clear say you can hear forever.

The Replay

Student: Professor, could you help me retrieve my camera? I've dropped it in the pool.

Professor: Certainly, but I'm completely dressed. Why not ask someone in the pool?

Student: Well, I've been told that you can go down deeper, stay down longer, and come up drier than anyone else!

LISTENING SKILL NO. 74
Laugh and Listen

The Action

Can humor enhance the listening process? Comedian Victor Borge says, "Humor is the shortest distance between two people." Occasional light touches do seem to bring people closer. How many sales have been clinched by a diverting, relaxing line? How many important points have been recalled because they were drolly depicted? How often has a touch of chaos been defused by a bit of wit? One-liners do backfire when a listener fails to fire back. Then it's so quiet you can hear a pun flop. Well, try again. Nothing succeeds better than failure.

The Replay

The more you strive to be sensible and serious and meaningful, the less chance you have of becoming so. The primary objective is to laugh.

—JOHN D. MACDONALD
Free Fall in Crimson

LISTENING SKILL NO. 75
Exercise Care with Arousal Words

The Action

Psychologist John Lavach suggests that when we include high-arousal words in conversation, we inhibit immediate memory while possibly enhancing longer-range recall. High-arousal words can be crudities, heresies, or profanities. Depending upon use, innocuous words can also arouse. To a dairy farmer, the word *margarine* can be disconcerting, as is *bank* to a savings-and-loan officer, *telephone pole* to a utility lineman, or *motorboat* to one who sails. We can care for our listeners by actively avoiding unsettling words, unless we want our listeners to remember what we said later. Keep in mind, however, that they will remember by associating our arousal words with our message—an interesting risk.

The Replay

Venerable saw: Actions speak louder than words.
Exception to the venerable saw: It depends upon who says what words where, when, to whom, at what volume, and with what intent.

LISTENING SKILL NO. 76
Be There to Hear

The Action

This book would surely be incomplete without putting to rest, once and for all, a dilemma that has intrigued us for centuries: If a tree falls in a forest and nobody is there to hear it, does it make any sound? You deserve a definite response, so here it is: Well, it depends. If you define sound as "the sensation of hearing," then you need to be there. If, however, you define sound as "mechanical radiant energy carried along longitudinal pressure waves," then it doesn't matter whether you're there or not. But then, if you're not there, how do you really know?

The Replay

Now that we've finally clarified *that,* what's the sound of one hand clapping?

LISTENING SKILL NO. 77
Listen—and Live

The Action

A failure to listen can be fatal. In *A Night to Remember,* Walter Lord's definitive account of the final hours of the ship *Titanic,* he recounts an exchange in the wireless shack. Purportedly, Second Operator Harold Bride suggested to First Operator John Phillips, "Send SOS; it's the new call, and it may be your last chance to send it." And so it was that at 12:45 A.M. on April 15, 1912, the first-ever SOS distress call was dispatched. Unfortunately, *Titanic* officers had chosen to ignore several earlier ice warnings sent over the wireless—decisions which ultimately led to the need for a distress call. It is always important to listen, even though such dire situations are rare. We trust we will never need to face a last-chance opportunity to use this essential skill.

The Replay

Q: "What's this?"
A: "It's a hand grenade."
Q: "How does it work?"
A: "You pull the pin and throw it."
Q: "Like this?"
A: "No! You throw the *grenade*—not the pin!"
(End of conversation)

LISTENING SKILL NO. 78
Assess the Odds

The Action

Few professional baseball players retire with lifetime batting averages of .300. Even superstars sometimes fail to hit safely during seven out of every ten official plate appearances. Football quarterbacks fare no better. At least six things can happen when a football is tossed toward an intended receiver. Five outcomes are unintended: a reception for no gain or loss, an interception, an offensive penalty, a fumble, or an incompleted pass. Similarly, our intended messages strike out, are received with no gain, are fumbled, or are charged with errors seventy-five percent of the time. Of course, we *receive* messages with equal inefficiency. While knowing the odds lends us slight comfort, it does give us more respect for the successful completions.

The Replay

The Listening Law of Three-Fourths:

1. Three-fourths of our workday is consumed by talking and listening activity;
2. Three-fourths of what we hear, we hear imprecisely; and
3. Three-fourths of what we hear accurately, we forget within three weeks.

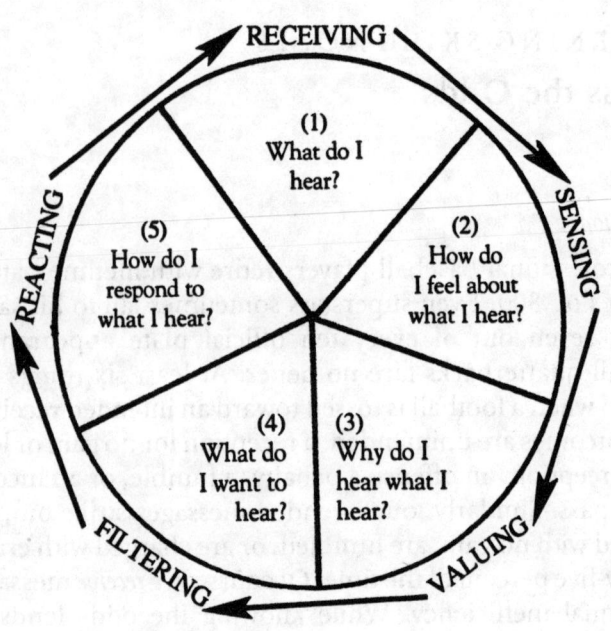

LISTENING SKILL NO. 79
Help Yourself

The Action

We've discussed five basic internal listening functions: receiving, sensing, valuing, filtering, and reacting. Listening Cycle I graphically depicts these functions (see illustration at left).

LISTENING CYCLE I—THE INTERNAL FUNCTIONS

These five questions remain as keys to the *internal* acceptance of, processing of, and response to auditory data.

The Replay

I can learn to help myself listen to you more effectively.

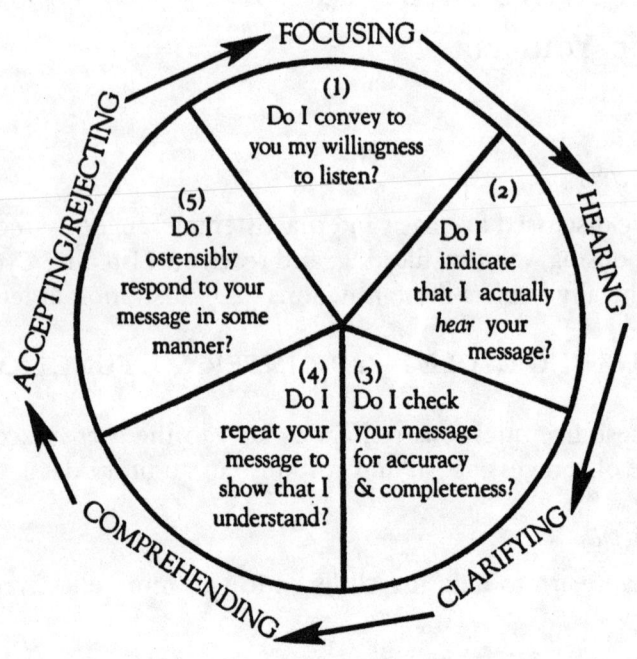

LISTENING SKILL NO. 80
Help the Speaker

The Action

We've discussed five basic *external* listening functions: focusing, hearing, clarifying, comprehending, and accepting/rejecting. Listening Cycle II graphically depicts these functions (see illustration at left).

LISTENING CYCLE II—THE EXTERNAL FUNCTIONS

These five questions remain as keys to the *external* acceptance of, processing of, and response to auditory data.

The Replay

I can learn to help you to help me listen more effectively.

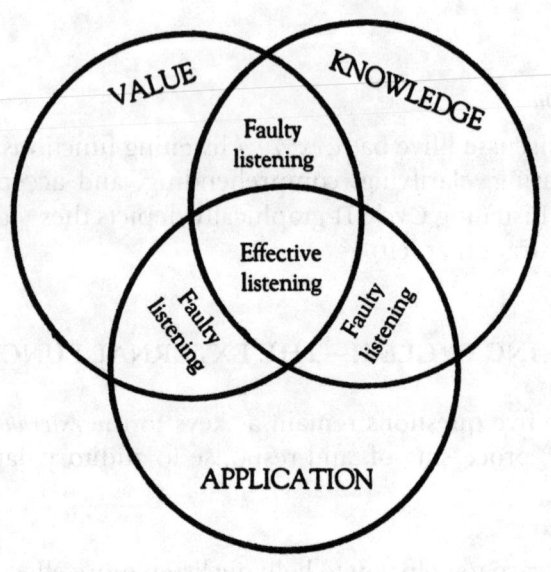

LISTENING SKILL NO. 81
Adopt Listening Skills for Lifetime Use

The Action

Effective listening includes three components:
1. Value—the placing of a high personal priority upon the importance of listening;
2. Knowledge—the possessing of certain listening techniques; and
3. Application—the active practicing of listening skills.

Encircling these components we have the illustration at left.

Note that "owning" only one or two of the components ensures faulty listening. For example, acknowledging the importance of listening (value) and having a willingness to practice certain skills (application) without understanding workable techniques (knowledge) produces a trial-and-error, though well-intended, approach. Other pairings are similarly faulty. Only when all components overlap can we have effective listening for lifetime use.

The Replay

The formula for effective listening:
$V + K + A = G - P$
Value plus Knowledge plus Application = Gain minus Pain

LISTENING SKILL NO. 82
Market Listening—It Pays!

The Action

The Sperry Corporation is credited with awakening an otherwise dormant interest in the importance of listening. Company commercials, advertisements, and internal seminars for managers stress that "listening can improve your vision." One such ad notes that "few see as far or as clearly as those who listen well." If we were to market listening, our ads might well read: Listening is a gift you give someone. It has no strings attached, requires no credit, costs nothing, is risk-free, yields high interest, is readily available, and benefits you both. And anyone can start a franchise. Interested? Inquire within.

The Replay

Things were so bad on Wall Street that when E. F. Hutton spoke nobody listened.

—JOHNNY CARSON

LISTENING SKILL NO. 83
Practice Today for Proficiency Tomorrow

The Action

A lingering myth about the skill of listening suggests that we already know what we need to know. Actually, few of us ever really master all of the listening skills we need for effective communication. Few hands are raised when participants in seminars on interpersonal skills are asked, "How many of you have listening problems?" However, when questioned further about recent listening errors, difficulty recalling verbal directions, or misinterpretations of what someone said, all but those who believe they walk on water acknowledge their less-than-perfect ability. This personal admission is an initial step in dispelling the myth. An "I can learn to listen more effectively" replaces the "I've already heard it all." Effective listening is a lifetime pursuit. Instant miracles are rare.

The Replay

Walking on water wasn't built in a day.

—JACK KEROUAC

LISTENING SKILL NO. 84
Probe Periodically

The Action

By using a periodic checkup approach, we can informally gauge our listening competence. Select a friend or colleague with whom you interact frequently. Invest twenty uninterrupted minutes and, each in turn, candidly answer these questions:

1) On a 1-to-10 scale, how do you rate me as a listener?
2) Can you recall any specific situations when I apparently wasn't listening to you?
3) Do I usually give you my full attention when you're talking?
4) Do you generally feel comfortable in talking with me?
5) Do I ever cut you off, appear to be disinterested, or avoid eye contact?
6) Am I usually open to your feedback? Do I sometimes react defensively?
7) Do you feel that I'm genuinely interested in you as well as what you are saying?
8) When you feel I'm not listening, are you willing to tell me *at that moment?*
9) Do you have any specific listening suggestions for me now?
10) Would you be willing to do this again in two months?

You can, of course, add to or delete from this list. What's important is that you and your friend or colleague begin refining each other's listening skills.

The Replay

Only when I can listen to you about me can I know myself better.